PASSIVE INCOME

Unlock the Potential of Your Money

Philipp Frühwirth

CONTENTS

INTRODUCTION TO PASSIVE INCOME

Everybody who works for an income dreams of a day when they can earn money without actively working. This is where passive income comes into play. Passive income is money that you earn without having to put in constant effort or time. You receive income regardless of whether or not you're working, and it can continue to flow in for a long time, even after you've stopped working.

Passive income is particularly appealing because it allows you to have more control over your time, to increase your income, and to achieve financial freedom quicker than if you're solely reliant on one source of income. With the right strategies and knowledge, anyone can generate passive income streams that help them achieve financial freedom.

Passive income comes in various forms, such as rental income, dividend income, capital gains, interest income, and more. It is important to understand the different types of passive income as they all require different levels of work and investment.

The key to gaining passive income is to build a source of income that is self-sustaining. This means that the source of income is scalable and doesn't require your constant attention, thus freeing up more time to build additional sources of income.

While passive income is achievable, it requires specialized knowledge and effort from the outset. It's important to understand that the term 'passive' can be misleading, as it takes time, effort, and investment to get started on the right track. Often, you'll need to work harder in the beginning stages of setting up a passive income stream than in any other stage.

Furthermore, it's important to be aware that generating passive income isn't a magic solution that can solve all your financial problems overnight. It takes time and a lot of effort to build it into a sustainable source of income. You must be prepared to learn, work, and be consistent in your efforts.

So, whether you're a business owner looking for ways to monetize your existing assets, or if you're just wanting to create an additional income stream, there are many methods that can help you achieve your goal of passive income. By applying yourself to the knowledge provided in this ebook, you too can generate passive income streams and achieve your financial goals.

TYPES OF PASSIVE INCOME

Passive income is a great way to earn money without having to actively work for it. It can be defined as any type of income that is earned with little to no effort on the part of the earner. There are many different types of passive income, and in this chapter, we'll be exploring some of the most popular ones.

Dividend Income:

One of the most common types of passive income is dividend income. This type of income is earned by investing in stocks that pay dividends to their shareholders. Dividends are typically paid out on a quarterly basis, and the amount of the dividend is determined by the company's board of directors. Dividend income can be a great way to earn passive income, especially if you invest in high-quality companies that have a long track record of paying dividends.

Real Estate Income:

Another popular type of passive income is real estate income. This can come in the form of rental income, where you rent out a property to tenants and collect monthly rent payments, or it can come in the form of capital gains, where you buy a property and sell it for a profit. Real estate can be a great way to generate passive income, but it does require a significant upfront investment.

Interest Income:

Interest income is another type of passive income that is earned by investing in interest-bearing accounts such as savings accounts, CDs, and bonds. The amount of interest earned depends on the interest rate and the amount invested. While interest income may not be the most exciting way to earn passive income, it can be a great way to earn a consistent stream of income.

Royalties:

If you're a creative type, you may be able to earn passive income through royalties. This type of income is earned by creating something that can be licensed or sold, such as a book, music, or software. Royalties are typically a percentage of the revenue earned from the product, and can be a great way to earn passive income if you have a product that is in high demand.

Affiliate Marketing:

Finally, affiliate marketing is another popular way to earn passive income. This is where you promote someone else's product or service and earn a commission for every sale that is made through your referral link. Affiliate marketing can be a great way to earn passive income, especially if you have a large audience that is interested in the products or services that you are promoting.

In conclusion, there are many different types of passive income, and each one has its own set of advantages and disadvantages. By exploring the different options and finding the right one for you, you can start earning passive income and take steps towards achieving financial freedom.

BENEFITS OF PASSIVE INCOME

Passive Income generally refers to the money earned without being actively involved in generating it. It is earnings derived from an enterprise in which a person is not materially involved. The benefits of passive income are numerous, and any individual can significantly supplement their financial well-being through passive income streams. Below are some of the benefits of passive income:

1. Financial Freedom: Passive income is a crucial factor for achieving financial independence. It enables you to break free from the cycle of trading time for money, thereby allowing you to have more time to focus on the things that matter most to you. With passive income, you can enjoy financial freedom, enjoy vacations, and choose to work or not, based on your needs.

2. Diversification of Income: Passive income is an excellent way to diversify your income sources. Relying on only one income source, such as a traditional job, can be risky. Job security is often uncertain, and layoffs or firings can happen with little warning, leaving individuals in financial hardship. Passive income streams create a safety net to avoid an over-reliance on a single income source.

3. Supplemental Income: Passive income streams serve as an excellent supplement to the regular income you earn from your job or other sources. Passive income provides additional cash flow, providing money to invest in other passive income businesses or investment options.

4. Making Money while Sleeping: Passive income streams allow you to make money even while sleeping, travelling or vacationing. Once you have set up a sound passive income stream, it continues

generating passive income with minimal effort, freeing you up to enjoy the rest of your time.

5. Financial Security: Passive income streams provide some level of financial security. They offer an additional cash-cushion in case of emergencies or unexpected events such as job-loss or medical emergencies. Passive income streams provide a sense of financial security and long-term sustainability.

6. Tax Benefits: Some forms of passive income, such as rental income and capital gains on investments, offer favorable tax rates compared to the ordinary earned income tax rate. It provides an opportunity to benefit from legal strategies to minimize tax liability.

In summary, passive income provides numerous benefits. It enables you to diversify and supplement your income, potentially provide financial security, attain financial freedom while reducing the burdening pressures of trading time for money. The following chapter explores the types of passive income streams available for individuals to create a more secure financial future.

SETTING SMART PASSIVE INCOME GOALS

Setting smart goals is an essential step when it comes to building passive income streams. It's important to define your goals, understand your motivation, and create a realistic action plan that you can stick to. In this chapter, we'll discuss how to set smart passive income goals that can help you achieve financial freedom.

Specific: The first step in setting smart passive income goals is to be specific about what you want to achieve. Instead of saying, "I want to make more money," try changing it to "I want to make $X amount of passive income per month." Having specific goals will motivate you to take the necessary actions to achieve them.

Measurable: Next, your goals have to be measurable. It's essential to track your progress regularly and ensure that you're heading in the right direction. You can measure your passive income stream through tools like spreadsheets or financial apps. By tracking your progress, you can identify areas that need improvement and tweak your plan accordingly.

Achievable: Your passive income goals must be achievable. It is important to set realistic expectations and goals that you can achieve. Setting unattainable targets can hinder your progress and cause you to lose motivation. Determine how much you can realistically make from each income stream, and set achievable goals that will keep you motivated and allow you to achieve success.

Relevant: Your passive income goals should be relevant to your overall financial goals. Determine what you want to achieve financially, and align your passive income goals accordingly.

Everyone's financial situation is different, so ensure that your goals fit your personal financial needs.

Time-bound: Finally, your goals should be time-bound. Having deadlines for your goals will help you stay focused and accountable. Establishing timelines and breaking your goals into smaller steps will keep you motivated and help you see progress along the way.

In conclusion, setting smart passive income goals is an important step in building a successful passive income stream. Remember to create specific, measurable, achievable, relevant, and time-bound goals that align with your overall financial goals. By doing so, you'll be able to achieve financial freedom and the passive income you desire.

STEPS TO BUILDING A
PASSIVE INCOME STREAM

Are you tired of the 9 to 5 job grind and looking for a way to build wealth, create financial freedom, and live life on your own terms? Building a passive income stream may be the solution for you. Passive income is money earned with little to no active involvement or time, allowing you to make money while you sleep. Here are some steps to build your own passive income stream:

Step 1: Choose the Right Passive Income Stream

The first step is to decide on a passive income stream that fits your skills, interests, and financial goals. Some popular passive income streams include rental properties, dividend stocks, mutual funds, e-commerce stores, affiliate marketing, and digital products such as books and courses.

Step 2: Develop a Business Plan

Once you have decided on a passive income stream, you should develop a business plan. This should include an overview of the business, marketing strategies, financial projections, and goals. A well-thought-out business plan will help you stay focused and motivated throughout the process.

Step 3: Set Realistic Goals

Setting realistic goals is critical to your success. Determine the amount of passive income you want to earn and set a deadline for achieving this goal. Be specific and measurable with your goals, and break them down into achievable milestones to track your progress.

Step 4: Build a Passive Income Portfolio

Building a diversified portfolio of passive income streams is essential. By spreading your investments across multiple sources, you reduce your risk and increase the potential for higher returns. Consider investing in real estate, dividend stocks, and digital products to create a well-rounded portfolio.

Step 5: Automate Your Business

Automation is key to building a passive income stream. Implement systems and tools that help automate your business operations and reduce the amount of hands-on work required. Use tools like social media schedulers, email marketing automation software, and project management tools to streamline your workflow.

Step 6: Monitor and Adjust

Finally, it is essential to monitor your progress regularly and make adjustments as needed. Keep track of your income streams' performance to identify areas of improvement and adjust your strategies accordingly. Review your business plan regularly and update it based on changes in your goals and market trends.

Conclusion

Building a passive income stream is a great way to create wealth and financial freedom over time. It requires dedication, hard work, and a long-term perspective, but the payoff can be substantial. By following these steps, you can begin to create a passive income stream that works for you and your financial goals.

INVESTING IN INDEX
FUNDS AND ETFS

Index funds and exchange-traded funds (ETFs) have become increasingly popular options for investors seeking a passive form of investment. Both index funds and ETFs offer investors the opportunity to invest in a diversified portfolio of stocks, bonds, or a combination of both without the need for extensive research and analysis.

Index funds and ETFs are designed to track the performance of a specific index. For example, the S&P 500 is an index that tracks the performance of 500 large-cap US stocks. An index fund or ETF that tracks the S&P 500 will invest in the 500 stocks in the same proportion as its weightage in the index.

One of the major benefits of investing in index funds or ETFs is their low expense ratios. Since they are passively managed, they do not require extensive research or frequent trading, resulting in lower management fees compared to actively managed funds. This makes them an attractive option for investors looking for low-cost and low-maintenance investments.

Another advantage of investing in index funds and ETFs is their diversification benefits. By investing in a broad range of stocks or bonds across different sectors and geographies, investors can reduce their portfolio risk and increase returns over the long term.

Furthermore, index funds and ETFs are highly liquid, making them easy to buy and sell on the stock exchange. Investors can trade these funds at any time during market hours, allowing for greater control and flexibility in investment decisions.

However, index funds and ETFs are not without their drawbacks. One of the biggest concerns for some investors is that they provide broad exposure to the market, which may not be suitable if an investor is seeking targeted exposure to specific sectors, industries, or companies. Additionally, in volatile market conditions, index funds and ETFs can perform poorly, resulting in losses for investors.

In conclusion, investing in index funds and ETFs can be an excellent option for investors looking for a low-cost, low-maintenance, diversified, and flexible investment option. However, as with any investment, it is important for investors to review their investment objectives, risk tolerance, and overall financial situation before investing.

INVESTING IN RENTAL PROPERTIES FOR PASSIVE INCOME

Investing in rental properties has long been a popular way to earn passive income. Owning a rental property can provide a steady stream of income and build long-term wealth. In this chapter, we will discuss the advantages of investing in rental properties, how to get started, and how to manage your rental property.

Advantages of Investing in Rental Properties

One of the most significant advantages of investing in rental properties is the potential for passive income. As a landlord, you can generate rental income that covers your expenses and provides you with a steady stream of cash flow. Additionally, property values tend to appreciate over time, meaning you can build wealth by holding onto your property long-term.

Investing in rental properties also allows for tax benefits. Rental property owners can deduct expenses related to the property, such as mortgage interest, property taxes, insurance, and repairs, from their taxable income. Additionally, rental income is considered passive income, meaning it is subject to a lower tax rate than active income.

Getting Started with Rental Properties

Before investing in rental properties, it is necessary to do your research and create a plan. Start by obtaining financing preapproval from a lender to determine how much you can afford, then research potential properties to invest in. Consider factors such as location, surrounding amenities, market trends, and tenant demand.

Once you have a property, it is necessary to set a rent rate and create a lease agreement. To set the rent rate, research other rental properties in the area to compare prices. A lease agreement should include the terms of the tenancy, such as rent amount, lease duration, and any pet policies.

Managing Rental Properties

Managing a rental property can be time-consuming, but it is necessary to ensure the property is profitable and well-maintained. A good property manager can take care of tasks such as screening tenants, handling repairs and maintenance, and collecting rent.

If you choose to manage the property yourself, it is essential to stay organized and keep detailed records. Keep receipts for all expenses related to the property and document any repairs or maintenance performed.

In conclusion, investing in rental properties can be an excellent way to generate passive income and build long-term wealth. However, it is crucial to do your research and have a solid plan before diving into the market. By managing your property effectively, you can enjoy the benefits of passive income without sacrificing valuable time and effort.

ONLINE BUSINESS IDEAS FOR PASSIVE INCOME

The internet has created a wealth of opportunities for individuals to generate passive income. Here are some online business ideas you can explore:

1. Affiliate Marketing: Affiliate marketing involves promoting other people's products and earning a commission for each sale you make. You can promote affiliate products using a blog, social media, or email marketing. Amazon's affiliate program is one of the most popular, but there are many other affiliate programs in various niches.

2. E-commerce: Running an online store can generate significant passive income if you get it right. You can create a dropshipping store, which involves selling products without holding inventory. Another option is to sell digital products such as ebooks, online courses, and printables.

3. Blogging: Blogging is a popular way to generate passive income online. You can monetize your blog through affiliate marketing, sponsored posts, display ads, and selling digital products.

4. YouTube: If you have a passion for creating videos, you can make money through YouTube. You can monetize your videos through ads, sponsored content, and affiliate marketing.

5. Podcasting: Podcasting has seen significant growth in recent years, and it's a great way to create passive income. You can monetize your podcast through sponsorships, affiliate marketing, and selling digital products.

6. Selling Stock Photos: If you have photography skills, you can sell

your photos online through stock photo sites such as Shutterstock and iStockPhoto. Every time someone downloads your photo, you earn a commission.

7. Online Courses: Creating online courses is another way to generate passive income. You can create courses on various topics, including business, marketing, and personal development.

8. App Development: If you have coding skills, creating mobile apps can generate significant passive income. You can sell your app on the App Store or Google Play Store or monetize it through ads or in-app purchases.

9. Membership Sites: Creating a membership site can be a lucrative way to generate passive income. You can offer exclusive content, courses, and community support to paid members.

In conclusion, generating passive income through online businesses requires time, effort, and the right strategies. You can start small and scale up as you gain experience and grow your audience. Choose an online business that aligns with your interests and skills, and be persistent in your efforts to succeed.

MAXIMIZING AFFILIATE MARKETING FOR PASSIVE INCOME

Affiliate marketing is one of the most popular ways to make passive income online. The basic idea behind affiliate marketing is that you promote someone else's products, and when someone buys through your unique affiliate link, you earn a commission. The commission amount can vary, depending on the product or service you're promoting, and sometimes it can be as high as 50% or more.

If you're interested in affiliate marketing, here are some tips to help you maximize your earnings:

1. Choose the Right Program

There are literally thousands of affiliate programs out there, so it's important to choose the right one that matches your niche and interests. When choosing an affiliate program to join, look for products or services that you are familiar with, or that align with your website or blog's niche. Also, make sure to read the fine print to ensure that the program's terms and conditions are favorable for your goals.

2. Know Your Audience

Understanding your audience's needs and interests is crucial when it comes to promoting affiliate products. You should create content that provides valuable information related to the product, in a way that is engaging to your audience. If your audience trusts you, they are more likely to click your affiliate links and purchase the product you are promoting.

3. Promote Quality Products

Your reputation as a blogger or content creator is vital to your long-term success in affiliate marketing. If you promote low-quality products, it won't take long for your readers to lose trust in you. So, make sure to only promote high-quality products or services, that you have personally used and stand behind.

4. Optimize Conversion Rates

Conversion rates refer to the percentage of visitors who click on your affiliate links and complete a purchase. To optimize your conversion rates, you can use effective call-to-action buttons, clear product descriptions, and appealing visuals. You can also offer discounts, bonuses, or other special offers to incentivize your audience to buy through your link.

5. Utilize Multiple Platforms

Promoting affiliate products through a single platform, such as your website or social media, can be limiting. To maximize your earnings, you should consider utilizing multiple platforms such as email marketing, podcasts, or even webinars to reach a wider audience and drive more traffic to your affiliate products.

In conclusion, affiliate marketing can be a lucrative source of passive income if you take the time to choose the right program, understand your audience, promote quality products, optimize conversion rates, and utilize multiple platforms. With these tips, you can start building a successful affiliate marketing strategy and earn passive income.

SELLING DIGITAL PRODUCTS FOR PASSIVE INCOME

The internet has opened up numerous opportunities for people to earn money passively by selling digital products. Digital products are any products that can be delivered electronically, such as e-books, videos, courses, templates, and software. By creating and selling digital products, you can generate passive income by leveraging your expertise in a particular field.

Here are some of the most popular digital products that you can sell for passive income:

1. E-books: E-books are a great way to share your knowledge with others and generate passive income at the same time. You can write an e-book on any topic that you are knowledgeable about, whether it's cooking, fitness, or business.

2. Video courses: Video courses are a popular way to sell digital products. They typically offer more in-depth information than e-books and can be used to teach a variety of skills, such as web design, programming, and marketing.

3. Templates: Templates are a great option for those who are proficient in graphic design or website design. They can include website templates, social media templates, business card templates, and more.

4. Software: If you have programming skills, you can create software that can solve a problem or make a task easier for someone. For example, a software that helps in scheduling social media posts or automating some other task.

5. Photography: If you're a photographer, you can sell digital

photos online. There are a number of websites that allow you to upload your photos and sell them to customers.

When it comes to selling digital products, there are a few platforms that can help you get started. One of the most popular platforms is Gumroad. Gumroad is a simple platform that allows you to upload and sell digital products. You can even set up a subscription plan to sell content on a recurring basis.

Another popular platform is Teachable. Teachable is a platform designed for creating and selling online courses. It allows instructors to create and manage their courses and even offers tools to market the courses to potential students.

When creating digital products, it's important to focus on providing high-quality content that addresses a specific need or interest. By doing so, you can attract a loyal customer base that will be willing to buy more of your products in the future. Additionally, you can promote your products through social media, email lists and other marketing channels to increase your visibility and sales.

In summary, selling digital products is an effective way to generate passive income. There's no limit to what you can create and sell, as long as there is a demand for your product. With the right platform and marketing strategy, you can turn your expertise into a profitable source of passive income.

BUILDING AN E-COMMERCE STORE FOR PASSIVE INCOME

An e-commerce store can provide an excellent source of passive income. All you need to do is set it up and let the sales roll in. However, building a successful e-commerce store requires more than just creating a website and filling it with products. Here are some steps you can take to build an e-commerce store that generates passive income.

1. Choose a Profitable Niche

The first step to building an e-commerce store is to choose a niche that is profitable. You should conduct market research to find out what products are in high demand and what competition you will face. Once you have identified a viable niche, you can start researching products that would appeal to your target market.

2. Select a Platform

The next step is to choose an e-commerce platform that suits your needs. Some popular options include Shopify, WooCommerce, BigCommerce, and Magento. Each has its pros and cons, so make sure to choose the one that aligns with your business goals and budget.

3. Create a Professional Website

Your website is the face of your business, so it's essential to invest in a professional website that exudes trust and credibility. Make sure your website is fast, mobile-responsive, and easy to navigate. You should also optimize it for search engines to start attracting organic traffic.

4. Develop High-Quality Product Listings

Your product listings should be detailed, descriptive, and engaging. Use high-quality photos and videos to showcase your products from different angles. Provide the necessary information, including product specifications, dimensions, and pricing.

5. Offer Competitive Pricing

Pricing is a crucial factor that can make or break your e-commerce store. You should research your competitors' pricing to ensure that you're offering competitive pricing. You could also use discounts and promotions to incentivize customers to make a purchase.

6. Use Email Marketing to Stay Connected

Email marketing is an excellent tool for staying connected with your customers and generating repeat business. You can use it to promote new products, offer exclusive discounts, and share relevant content to keep your customers engaged.

7. Expand Your Product Line

As your e-commerce store grows, consider expanding your product line to offer a wider range of products. You can also use analytics to identify your best-selling products and invest in those to maximize your profits.

In conclusion, building an e-commerce store is an excellent way to generate passive income. However, it requires careful planning, a solid business strategy, and quality execution. By following these steps, you can build a successful e-commerce store that generates passive income for years to come.

CREATING A COURSE FOR PASSIVE INCOME

Creating a course for passive income is a great way to leverage your knowledge and expertise into revenue. Whether you're passionate about business, marketing, personal development, or any other topic, you can turn your expertise into a profitable passive income stream. In this chapter, we'll cover how to create a successful course for passive income.

Step 1: Choosing a topic

The first step in creating a course is choosing a topic. It's important to choose a topic that you're knowledgeable about and that you're passionate about. This will ensure that you're motivated to create the course and that you'll be able to provide value to your students.

Step 2: Defining your audience

Once you have a topic in mind, you need to define your target audience. Who is your course for? What problems do they have that your course can solve? Understanding your audience is critical to creating a course that resonates with your students.

Step 3: Planning your course

When planning your course, break it down into manageable sections or lessons. Outline the content, objectives, and learning outcomes for each section. Consider how you'll deliver the content - will it be video lessons? Audio recordings? Written content? Make sure to include interactive elements such as quizzes, exercises, and assignments to keep your students engaged.

Step 4: Recording and editing your content

Once you have a plan for your course, it's time to start recording your content. Invest in quality equipment such as a good microphone and camera to ensure that your content is clear and professional-looking. Edit your recordings to remove any errors or awkward pauses and add music and graphics to create an engaging learning experience.

Step 5: Marketing your course

Once your course is complete, it's time to market it. Use social media to promote your course and run targeted ads to reach your target audience. Consider reaching out to influencers or bloggers in your niche to promote your course to their audience. You can also use affiliate marketing to encourage people to promote your course in exchange for a commission.

Step 6: Scaling your course

To maximize your passive income from your course, consider scaling it. You can create multiple courses or offer additional courses to students who have completed your initial course. You could also consider licensing your course to other online course platforms to reach a wider audience.

In conclusion, creating a course for passive income is a great way to monetize your expertise and knowledge. By choosing a topic you're passionate about, defining your audience, planning your course, recording and editing your content, marketing your course, and scaling your course, you can create a successful and profitable passive income stream.

PASSIVE INCOME THROUGH ADVERTISING

Passive income through advertising is a popular way to make money online that requires minimal effort once it is set up. It involves generating revenue from advertising space on your website or blog. Whenever visitors click on ads placed on your website or blog, you earn a commission. Many people have made a good living from this business model. In this chapter, we will explore how to make passive income through advertising.

#1. Set Up a Website or Blog
The first step to making money through advertising is to have a website or a blog. You could create one for free using platforms like WordPress, Wix or Weebly, or pay for a custom domain name and hosting service. Ensure that your website or blog is optimized for search engines and has quality content that would attract visitors.

#2. Choose the Right Advertising Network
The next step is to choose the right advertising network to work with. Google AdSense is a popular choice, but there are also other networks like Media.net, InfoLinks, and Chitika. Look for an advertising network that offers high commissions and has a good reputation.

#3. Optimize Your Ad Placement
Ad placement is crucial when it comes to earning passive income through advertising. You want to place your ads in strategic positions where they are most likely to be seen by visitors. The placement of your ads should be visually attractive but not too intrusive.

#4. Drive Traffic to Your Website

The more traffic your website or blog attracts, the higher your chances of earning passive income through advertising. You can drive traffic through social media, search engine optimization, and paid advertising. You should also ensure that your website's content is engaging enough to keep visitors coming back.

#5. Monitor Your Results

You need to monitor your website's analytics regularly to determine the effectiveness of your ad placement, website design, and content. This information will guide you on what changes to make to increase your earnings. You want to ensure that you are meeting the requirements of your advertising network and that your website's performance is optimized.

Conclusion

Passive income through advertising is a simple and effective way to generate income online. With the right strategies in place, you can earn a decent income from ad revenue. Remember to work with reputable advertising networks, optimize your ad placement, drive traffic to your website or blog, and regularly monitor your results to increase your earnings.

SELLING STOCK PHOTOS FOR PASSIVE INCOME

If you have a passion for photography, turning it into a passive income stream could be a great option. Stock photography is a popular way to earn passive income by selling your photos online.

In this chapter, we'll dive into selling stock photos for passive income, including the benefits of this method and how to get started.

Benefits of Selling Stock Photos for Passive Income
One of the primary benefits of selling stock photos is its passive nature. Once you upload your photos to stock photography websites, you earn money each time someone licenses your images. You don't have to continually market your photos or create new images to ensure a steady stream of income.

Another benefit of stock photography is that it allows you to earn money from photos you've taken in the past. Photographs can be a valuable asset if you sell them, and stock photography allows you to monetize your existing collection.

Moreover, because stock photo libraries serve customers from all over the globe, there's always a demand for photos of different subjects and styles. As long as you create high-quality, in-demand images and add them to reputable stock photo sites, you can see a good return on your investment.

How to Get Started with Selling Stock Photos
To get started with selling stock photos, you'll need to create high-quality images that meet the requirements of stock photography sites. You should research image requirements, such as minimum file size, image resolution, and image formats, before uploading

your photos to stock photography sites.

Then, you'll want to choose a stock photography site to work with. It's essential to research different stock photography sites to see which aligns best with your needs and goals as a photographer.

Once you've chosen a stock photography site, you'll need to upload your photos and keyword them. Keywords are essential for potential buyers to find your images, so make sure you use descriptive, specific keywords that accurately reflect the subject and style of your photos.

Once your photos are uploaded and keyworded, you can sit back and let your photos generate passive income for you. While it's unlikely that you'll see substantial income from selling stock photos alone, it's a low-maintenance method that can provide a steady stream of passive income over time.

Conclusion
Selling stock photos can be an excellent passive income stream for photographers. The demand for stock photos continues to grow exponentially, with businesses and bloggers always in need of high-quality images. If you love photography and want to turn it into a passive income stream, selling stock photos is a great place to start.

PASSIVE INCOME FROM YOUTUBE AND PODCASTING

In recent years, YouTube and podcasting have become popular forms of entertainment, information, and education. Along with their growing popularity, they have also become lucrative platforms for generating passive income. In this chapter, we will explore the avenues available to make money through YouTube and podcasting.

How to make passive income through YouTube

YouTube is a platform where people from all walks of life can share their creative ideas and content with a global audience. Once you establish a channel with a substantial following, there are multiple ways to leverage the platform to earn passive income.

One popular way to monetize your YouTube channel is through ads. YouTube pays you a share of ad revenue based on how many views your videos generate. While it may take some time and effort to create content that ranks high on YouTube's algorithms, once your channel begins to grow, it can become a lucrative source of passive income.

Another way to make money on YouTube is through sponsored content. Brands can sponsor your video, and in return, you showcase their products or services to your audience. This way, you earn a commission for every sale that may occur as a result of the endorsement.

Collaborating with other YouTubers or creating courses can also create a secondary stream of passive income. If you have expertise in a specific field, you can offer to conduct workshops or masterclasses for your audience. You can also write books or sell merchandise that incorporates your brand.

How to make passive income through Podcasting

Podcasting is another medium for creating passive income. Like YouTube, you can earn money through ads, sponsorships, merchandise, and collaborations.

Sponsorship and ads are the main sources of income for podcasters. You can collaborate with brands that are relevant to your podcast's niche, and the company pays you for every mention or endorsement of their product or service.

Merchandising is another strategy to tap into a growing podcast audience. By creating products specific to the niche topic of your podcast, you increase your chances of garnering attention and sales from your listeners.

Another strategy to monetize your podcast is through public speaking. If your podcast covers an area of expertise or popular news, you could receive invitations for speaking engagements. These pay significant sums, especially for topics that have a high demand.

Conclusion

Creating and growing a platform on YouTube or podcasting can take significant effort, but it is a powerful method of generating passive income. By leveraging the various methods of monetization available, you can create a substantial income stream that can continue to grow even as you work on other things.

INVESTING IN DIVIDEND STOCKS FOR PASSIVE INCOME

Investing in dividend stocks is another way to earn passive income. Dividends are payments made by companies to their shareholders as a reward for holding their stock. The amount paid is usually a percentage of the stock price, and the frequency of the payments can vary from monthly to annually. While not all companies pay dividends, many established and financially stable firms do.

Dividend stocks can provide investors with an ongoing stream of passive income. Companies that pay dividends typically have a long history of steady revenue growth and stable cash flows. As such, they are often considered relatively low-risk investments, particularly for those seeking regular income.

Here are some things to consider when investing in dividend stocks for passive income:

1. Look for companies with a long history of paying dividends.

Companies that have a track record of paying dividends consistently over many years are likely to continue doing so in the future. You can research a company's dividend history on financial websites like Yahoo Finance or Seeking Alpha.

2. Consider the dividend payout ratio.

The dividend payout ratio is the percentage of a company's earnings that are paid out as dividends. A higher dividend payout ratio means that more of the company's earnings are paid out as dividends. A lower payout ratio means that the company is retaining more of its earnings for other purposes. A sustainable dividend payout ratio is generally between 40% and 60% of earnings.

3. Evaluate the company's financial health.

It's important to look at a company's financials to ensure that it has the ability to continue paying dividends. Look at metrics like revenue growth, cash flow, and debt levels. A strong balance sheet is an indicator that a company is financially stable.

4. Diversify your portfolio.

As with any investment, it's important to diversify your dividend stock holdings. Spread your investments across different sectors and industries to minimize your risk.

5. Reinvest your dividends.

Reinvesting your dividends can help to compound your returns over time. Many brokerages offer automatic dividend reinvestment plans (DRIPs) that reinvest your dividends for you at no extra cost.

In conclusion, investing in dividend stocks can be a reliable way to earn passive income. By choosing quality companies with a track record of paying dividends, you can build a steady stream of income that can help you achieve your financial goals.

REAL ESTATE CROWDFUNDING FOR PASSIVE INCOME

Real estate crowdfunding involves multiple investors pooling their resources together to invest in a larger real estate project. This form of investment allows individuals to invest in real estate without buying physical property.

One of the benefits of crowdfunding is that it allows real estate investors to participate in larger projects that might otherwise be unavailable to them if they were investing on their own.

Here are some of the benefits of real estate crowdfunding:

Diversification: With real estate crowdfunding, individuals can invest in multiple properties with different levels of risk. Investors can take on low risk, stable projects or high-risk/high-reward projects.

Lower minimum investment: Compared to buying physical property, crowdfunding allows investors to add real estate to their investment portfolio with a lower minimum investment.

Low transaction costs: Investing in real estate comes with its own set of transaction costs such as stamp duty, loan application fees, and legal fees. However, with real estate crowdfunding, investors are usually not required to pay these fees.

Passive income: Real estate crowdfunding provides an opportunity to earn passive income through rental yields or capital appreciation. Investors can earn regular income through interest payments or dividend distributions.

Transparency: Crowdfunding platforms generally provide detailed information on each investment opportunity, including the risks and potential returns. Investors have access to due diligence reports and other data, which allows them to make more informed investment decisions.

No management responsibilities: When investing via a crowdfunding platform, investors do not need to worry about property management, maintenance or tenant relationships as these responsibilities are handled by the asset manager or sponsor.

Real estate crowdfunding, as with any investment, comes with its risks. Investors must do their due diligence, understand the risks involved and assess the potential returns before making any investment decisions.

In summary, real estate crowdfunding provides a low-cost, low-risk investment option for those looking for passive income from the real estate market. It allows investors to participate in real estate projects, even with small amounts of capital, providing them with an opportunity for diversification and stable returns.

PEER-TO-PEER LENDING FOR PASSIVE INCOME

Peer-to-peer (P2P) lending is a method of lending money to individuals or small businesses without going through a traditional financial institution. This process connects investors with borrowers through online lending platforms that facilitate the lending process. As a result, peer-to-peer lending offers investors the opportunity to earn passive income by earning interest on the loans they provide.

How P2P Lending Works

P2P lending platforms match investors with borrowers by considering the investor's risk tolerance, the borrower's credit score, and the loan amount. The platform will then assign an interest rate and term to the loan which will be used to calculate the investor's monthly return.

Investors can then review loan applications and choose the ones they want to invest in. Investors receive monthly principal and interest payments until the loan is repaid in full.

Benefits of P2P Lending

1. Passive Income Generation: P2P lending provides investors with a predictable stream of passive income. Investors can receive payments every month, depending on the loan term.

2. Diversification: P2P lending offers a way for investors to diversify their portfolios beyond traditional stocks and bonds.

3. Better Returns: P2P lending can offer higher yields than traditional fixed-income investments such as savings accounts, CDs, and bonds.

4. Control Over Investment: Investors can review the details of each loan and decide which ones to invest in. Investors can also choose the amount they want to invest, enabling them to build a diversified portfolio.

Risks of P2P Lending

1. Default Risk: Borrowers may default on their loans, and investors may lose part or all of their investment.

2. Market Risk: P2P lending does not have the same level of market regulation as traditional investments, which may expose investors to additional risks.

3. Liquidity Risk: Unlike stocks, bonds, or mutual funds, P2P loans are not easily tradable.

4. Limited Historical Data: P2P lending is a relatively new investment that does not yet have a long track record for investors to assess.

Conclusion

Peer-to-peer lending is a growing industry that can provide investors with a way to earn passive income by lending to individuals and small businesses. P2P lending offers investors the potential for higher yields than traditional fixed-income investments, but it also comes with risks that investors should consider. Ultimately, peer-to-peer lending can be a valuable addition to a diversified investment portfolio.

SCALING YOUR PASSIVE INCOME FOR FINANCIAL FREEDOM.

Passive income can be a great way to create long-term financial stability and achieve financial freedom. While earning passive income can require some upfront effort, once the income streams are established, they can continue to generate income for years. After creating and optimizing some passive income streams, you can start scaling them to increase your earnings and create a higher level of financial freedom. In this chapter, we will discuss some useful strategies and tools for scaling your passive income and achieving financial freedom.

1. Outsource tasks: As your passive income streams grow, it can become inefficient to manage all of the tasks involved in maintaining them, especially if you are still working full-time. To maximize your time, consider outsourcing tasks like content creation, social media management, and customer service to freelancers or virtual assistants.

2. Diversify your investments: Diversification is crucial for a successful passive income strategy. Consider adding new passive income streams, such as investing in dividend stocks, real estate crowdfunding, creating an e-commerce store, or peer-to-peer lending. Diversification can help you reduce the risk of losing all your passive income if one stream fails.

3. Automate your systems: Automation can save you a lot of time and energy in maintaining and growing your passive income streams. Automate tasks like billing, bill payments, and product delivery by setting up systems and platforms that allow you to

focus on growing your streams.

4. Invest in education: To achieve financial freedom, investing in your education is crucial. You can learn more about passive income streams, investing, and other financial topics through books, courses, and seminars.

5. Surround yourself with like-minded people: Building relationships with other people who have similar goals and are pursuing passive income can accelerate your growth. Attend networking events, conferences, and seminars designed for passive income entrepreneurs to build a network of supportive like-minded people.

In conclusion, achieving financial freedom through passive income takes dedication and hard work, but by scaling your passive income streams, you can increase your earnings and create a more stable financial future. Remember to diversify your investments, automate your passive income streams, outsource tasks, invest in education, and surround yourself with supportive like-minded people to achieve your goals.